Nudity

Liberty

Back

DUTY

eavesdrop

frog

Overwork

KT-484-013

ainting

guilt

His

Riches

Antipathy

ZEAL

Indiscreti

VITUPERATION

happiness

Misfor

loquacity

English

WAR

Clergyman

Diplomacy

LOVE

Saint

MOUTH

Cat

Krishna

Mammon

mouse

felon

Bachelor

LAUGHTER

Vanity

habit

Omen

Garter

talk

NOISE

zenith

GOLD

Quack

Succe:

hedgehog

Dad

Politeness

Cal

KLEPTOMANIA

Rash

Egotist

Authentic

vhite

Language

the shorter
Devil's Dictionary

Appletree Press

First published in 1998 by
The Appletree Press Ltd,
19-21 Alfred Street,
Belfast, BT2 8DL
Tel: +44 (0) 1232 243074
Fax: +44 (0) 1232 256756
Web Site: www.irelandseye.com
E-mail: frontdesk@appletree.ie

The Shorter Devil's Dictionary

A catalogue for this book is available from the
British Library.

ISBN 0-86281-632-7

9 8 7 6 5 4 3 2 1

introduction

Ambrose Bierce began *The Devil's Dictionary* in an American weekly paper in 1881, and it rapidly gained renown. In fact, many of its sharp and original definitions became so widely quoted that the author himself was accused of plagiarising them.

Bierce was an enemy to every form of cant, hypocrisy, soft-selling, eulogy, jargon, prosiness, blind optimism and sentimentality. He looked at the foibles and weaknesses of humanity with a piercing and unforgiving eye, and addressed his dictionary to those enlightened souls who prefer dry wines to sweet, sense to sentiment, wit to humour, and clean English to slang.

This book presents a selection from *The Devil's Dictionary*, long enough to provoke thoughtful smiles, short enough to avoid tedium.

Adore To venerate expectantly.

air

A nutritious substance supplied by a bountiful Providence for the fattening of the poor.

the shorter Devil's Dictionary

Alone In bad company.

Ambidextrous Able to pick a pocket with either hand.

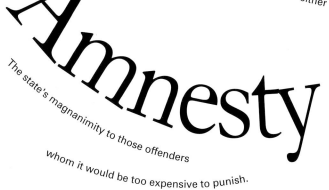

Amnesty The state's magnanimity to those offenders whom it would be too expensive to punish.

7

Antipathy

The sentiment inspired by one's friend's friend.

APOLOGISE

To lay the foundations for a future offence.

archbishop

An ecclesiastical dignitary one point holier than a bishop.

ARCHITECT

One who drafts a plan
of your house,
and plans a draft of your money.

Armour

The kind of clothing worn by a man
whose tailor is a blacksmith.

ass

A public singer with a good voice but no ear.

Authentic

Indubitably
true - in
somebody's
opinion.

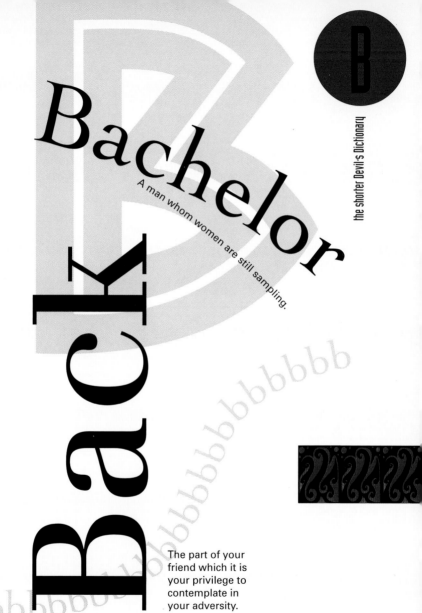

B

Bachelor

A man whom women are still sampling.

Back

The part of your friend which it is your privilege to contemplate in your adversity.

Backbite

To speak of a man as you find him when he can't find you.

ballot

A simple device by which a majority proves to a minority the folly of resistance.

barber

A savage whose laceration of your cheek is unobserved in the superior torment of his conversation.

bastinado

The art of walking on wood without exertion.

Beauty

The power by which a woman charms a lover and terrifies a husband.

BEFRIEND

To make an ingrate.

begger

A pest
unkindly
inflicted upon
the suffering
rich.

14

BETRAY

Bigot

One who is obstinately attached to an opinion that you do not entertain.

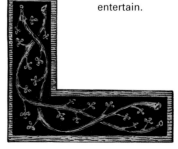

To make payment for confidence.

Bore

A person who talks when you wish him to listen.

Bottle-nosed

Having a nose created in the image of its maker.

BRAIN

An apparatus with which we think that we think.

Bride

A woman with a fine prospect of happiness behind her.

Cab

A tormenting vehicle in which a pirate jolts you through devious ways to the wrong place, where he robs you.

CANNIBAL

A gastronome of the old school.

CAROUSE

To celebrate with appropriate ceremonies the birth of a noble headache.

Cat

A soft, indestructible automaton provided by Nature to be kicked when things go wrong in the domestic circle.

Christen

To seek another's approval of a course of action already decided on.

19

C

the shorter Devil's Dictionary

Christmas

A day consecrated to gluttony, drunkeness, maudlin sentiment, gift-taking, public dullness and domestic behaviour.

CIRCUS

A place where horses, ponies and elephants are permitted to see men, women and children acting the fool.

20

Clergyman

A man who undertakes the management of our spiritual affairs as a method of bettering his temporal ones.

Commerce

A kind of transaction in which A plunders from B the goods of C, and for compensation B picks the pocket of D of money belonging to E.

Congratulations

The civility of envy.

Consult

To seek another's approval of a course of action already decided on.

Connoisseur

Someone who knows everything about something and nothing about anything else.

C

Coward

cccccccccccccccc

One who in an emergency thinks with his legs.

Cynic

A blackguard whose faulty vision sees things as they are, and not as they ought to be.

Dad

A father whom his vulgar children do not respect.

dawn The time when men of reason go to bed.

day A period of twenty-four hours mostly mis-spent.

Debauchee

One who has so earnestly pursued pleasure that he has had the misfortune to overtake it.

Deliberation

The act of examining one's bread to see what side it is buttered on.

Deserve

The quality of being entitled to what somebody else obtains.

diplomacy

The patriotic art of lying for one's country.

Distance

The only thing that the rich are willing for the poor to call theirs, and keep.

DUTY

That which sternly impels us in the direction of profit, along the lines of desire.

eavesdrop

Secretly to overhear a catalogue of the crimes and vices of another or yourself.

a snake to a pig, a pig to a man, and a man to a worm.

economy

Purchasing the barrel of whiskey you do not need for the price of the cow you cannot afford.

Edible

Good to eat, as a worm to a toad, a toad to a snake, a snake to a pig,

Egotist

A person of low taste more interested in himself than me.

E

eloquence A method of convincing fools.

English

A language so haughty and reserved that few writers succeed in getting on terms of familiarity with it.

err To believe or act in a way contrary to my beliefs and actions.

EXILE

One who serves by residing abroad, yet is not an ambassador.

felon

A person of greater enterprise than discretion.

fiddle

A instrument to tickle human ears by friction of a horse's tail on the entrails of a cat.

fidelity

A virtue peculiar to those who are about to be betrayed.

f

friendship

A ship big enough to carry two in fair weather, but only one in foul.

friendless

Having no favours to bestow.

frog

A reptile with edible eggs.

future

That period of time in which our affairs prosper, our friends are true and our happiness is assured.

Gambler

A man.

Garter

An elastic band intended to keep a woman from coming out of her stockings and desolating the country.

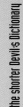

GENEALOGY

An account of one's descent from an ancestor who did not particularly care to trace his son.

G

GOLD

Formerly spelled 'God' - the 'L' was inserted to distinguish it from the name of another and inferior deity.

gratitude

The condition of one who is known to have committed an indiscretion, as distinguished from the state of him who has covered his tracks.

guilt

A sentiment lying midway between a benefit received and a benefit expected.

habit

A shackle for the free.

HAMMER

An instrument for smashing the human thumb.

happiness

An agreeable sensation arising from contemplating the misery of another.

the shorter Devil's Dictionary

haughty

Proud and disdainful, like a waiter.

HEDGEHOG

The cactus of the animal kingdom.

34

Hermit

A person whose vices and follies are not sociable.

His

Hers.

An account, mostly false, of events, mostly unimportant.

HISTORY

35

HOME

The place of last resort - open all night.

HOPE

Desire and expectation.

Hospitality

The virtue which induces us to feed and lodge persons who are not in need of food and lodging.

Husband

See Brute.

IMMIGRANT

An unenlightened person who thinks one country better than another.

Immoral

Inexpedient.

Incompatibility

In matrimony, a similarity of tastes, particularly the taste of domination.

Indiscretion

The guilt of a woman.

Inventor

A person who makes an ingenious arrangement of wheels, levers and springs, and believes it civilisation.

KILL

To create a vacancy without nominating a successor.

KILT

A costume worn by Scotchmen in America and Americans in Scotland.

Kindness A brief preface to ten volumes of exaction.

KING A male person commonly known in America as a 'crowned head'.

Kiss A word invented by the poets as a rhyme for 'bliss'.

KLEPTOMANIA A rich thief.

Krishna A form under which the pretended god Vishnu became incarnate. A very likely story indeed.

Language

The music with which we charm the serpents guarding another's treasure.

An interior convulsion, producing a distortion of the features and accompanied by inarticulate noises.

LAUGHTER

Law yer

One skilled in
circumvention
of the law.

LAZINESS

Unwarranted
repose of manner
in a person of low
degree.

LECTURER

One with
his hand in
your pocket,
his tongue
in your ear,
and his faith
in your
patience.

leisure

Lucid intervals in a disordered life.

libertine

Literally a free man; hence, one who is in bonds to his passions.

Liberty

One of Imagination's most precious possessions.

Litigation

A machine which you go into as a pig
and come out as a sausage.

A disorder which renders the sufferer unable to curb his tongue when you wish to talk.

loquacity

MAD

Affected by a high degree of mental independence.

A member of the unconsidered, or negligible sex. The genus has two varieties: good providers and bad providers.

male

Mammon

The god of the world's leading religion. His chief temple is in the holy city of New York.

Man

An animal so lost in rapturous contemplation of what he thinks he is, as to overlook what he indubitably ought to be. Infests the whole habitable earth and Canada.

Marvellous

Not understood.

mayonnaise

One of the sauces which serve the French in place of a state religion.

mediate

To butt in.

Meekness

Uncommon patience in planning a revenge that is worth while.

Mercy

An attribute beloved of detected offenders.

mine

Belonging to
me if I can hold
or seize it.

MINOR

Less objectionable.

Misfortune

The kind
of fortune
that never misses.

morning

The end of the night and dawn of dejection.

mouse

An animal that
strews its path
with fainting
women.

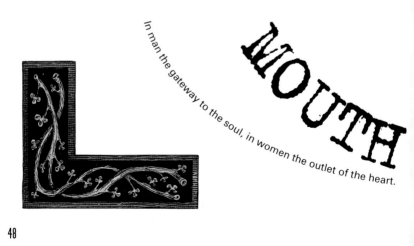

In man the gateway to the soul, in women the outlet of the heart.

MOUTH

Neighbour

One whom we are commanded to love as ourselves; and who does all he knows how to make us disobedient.

nepotism

Appointing your grandfather to office for the good of the party.

NOISE

The chief product and authenticating sign of civilisation.

Nominee

A modest gentleman shrinking from the distinction of private life and diligently seeking the honourable obscurity of public office.

NOTORIETY

The fame of one's competitor for public honours.

novel

A short story padded.

November

The eleventh twelfth of a weariness.

Nudity

That quality in art that is most painful to the prurient.

Omen

A sign that something will happen if nothing happens.

Once

Enough.

optimism

The belief that everything is right that is wrong.

Overwork

A dangerous disorder affecting high public functionaries who want to go fishing.

Outcome

A particular type of disappointment.

Painting

The art of protecting flat surfaces from the weather and exposing them to the critic.

Peace

In international affairs a period of cheating between two periods of fighting.

PHILOSOPHY

A route of many roads leading from nowhere to nothing.

A parlour utensil for subduing the impenitent visitor.

It is operated by depressing the keys of the machine and the spirits of the audience.

PIANO

PITIFUL

The state of
an enemy or
opponent,
after an
imaginary
encounter
with oneself.

platitude

The wisdom of
a million fools, all
that is mortal of
a departed truth.

Politeness

The most acceptable hypocrisy.

POLITICS

The conduct of public affairs for private advantage.

A species of geese indigenous to Portugal, mostly without feathers and imperfectly edible, even when stuffed with garlic.

Portuguese

P

Positive

Mistaken at the top of one's voice.

The only portion of a lady's letter which you need read if you are in a hurry.

postscript

precocious

A four-year old who elopes with his sister's doll.

PREDICT

To relate an

event that has

not occured, is

not ocurring

and will not

occur.

Prescription

A physician's guess at what will best prolong the treatment with the least harm to the patient.

ppppppppppppp

Primitive

People who believe that 'honesty is the best policy'.

PRINCIPAL

A subject which may be made very interesting, if well handled.

ppppppppppppppp

promise

This and good advice make an excellent gift, which we can all afford to give to the poor.

Quack

A murderer without a licence.

Quantity

A good substitute for quality when you go hungry.

Quorum

A sufficient number of members of a deliberative body to have their own way and their own way of having it.

QUOTATION

The act of repeating erroneously the words of another.

R

the shorter Devil's Dictionary

Radicalism

The conservation of tomorrow injected into the affairs of today.

Rash

Insensible to the value of our advice.

Reality

The dream of a mad philosopher.

REBEL

A proponent of a new misrule who has failed to establish it.

recollect

To recall with additions something not previously known.

Refreshing

Meeting a man who believes all he reads in the papers.

rent

An outrage, imposed by blood-sucking vampires on virtuous sons of toil.

Unable to leave.

resident

RESIGN

A good thing to do when you are going to be kicked out.

RESPONSIBILITY

A detached burden, easily shifted onto the shoulders of God, Fate, Fortune, Luck or one's neighbour.

Riches

The savings of many
in the hands of one.

S

Saint

A dead sinner revised and edited.

Sanity

A state of mind which immediately precedes and follows murder.

Sauce

The one infallible sign of civilisation and enlightenment.

Scribbler

A professional writer whose views are antagonistic to one's own.

Scripture

Obsolete in the pulpit - succumbed to by politics.

SELF

The most important person in the universe.

Selfish

Devoid of consideration for
the selfishness of others.

S

Self-evident

Evident to oneself and to no one else.

Success

The one unpardonable sign against one's fellow.

talk

To commit an
indiscretion without
temptation.

teetotaller

One who abstains from strong drink,
sometimes totally, sometimes
tolerably totally.

TRUTHFUL Dumb and illiterate.

twice Once too often.

Ugliness

A gift of the gods to certain women, entailing virtue without humility.

Ultimatum

In diplomacy, a last demand before resorting to concessions.

Un-American

Wicked, intolerable, heathenish. Cf Un-British, Un-Australian, etc.

Understanding

A cerebral secretion that enables one having it to know a house from a horse by the roof of the house.

UNIVERSALIST

One who forgoes the advantage of Hell for persons of another faith.

Urbanity

The kind of civility that urban observers ascribe to dwellers in all cities but New York.

usage

The First person of the literary Trinity, the Second and Third being Custom and Conventionality.

69

VALOUR A soldierly compound of vanity, duty and the gambler's hope.

Vanity

The tribute of the fool to the worth of the nearest ass.

Virtues Certain abstentions.

VITUPERATION

Satire, as understood by dunces and all such as suffer from an impediment in their wit.

Vote

The instrument and symbol of a freeman's power to make a fool of himself and a wreck of his country.

W

WAR

A ceremony at which two persons undertake to become one, one undertakes to become nothing, and nothing undertakes to become supportable.

A by-product of the arts of peace.

Wedding

Wheat

A cereal from which tolerably good whiskey can be made, and which is also used for bread.

white

Black.

Woman

An animal usually living in the vicinity of man, and having a rudimentary susceptibility to domestication.

ZEAL

A nervous disorder

afflicting the young

and inexperienced.

zenith

A point in the heavens directly overhead to a standing man or a growing cabbage.

Nudity Ugliness
Liberty Back DUTY eavesdrop frog Overwork
His
Painting guilt
Riches Antipathy ZEAL Indiscret happiness Misfo
VITUPERATION loquacity English happiness WAR
Clergyman
LOVE Diplomacy
MOUTH
Saint Cat
Krishna Mammon

mouse

Bachelor felor

LAUGHTER

Vanity

Omen

habit

Garter

NOISE

zenith

GOLD

talk

Quack

Succes

hedgehog

Politeness

Dad

KLEPTOMANIA

Cab

Rash

Egotist

Authentic

vhite

Language